TYPICAL EXAMPLES

OF

MODERN DREDGING MACHINERY

SELECTED FROM
RECENT DESIGNS BY

A. W. ROBINSON, M. INST. C. E.

SEA-GOING HOPPER DREDGE "FIELDING"
CAPACITY: 800 CUBIC YARDS PER HOUR DREDGING DEPTH, 52 FEET
A. W. ROBINSON, M. INST. C. E.
MONTREAL, CANADA

SEA-GOING ELEVATOR DREDGE "DENVER"
CAPACITY: 1 000 CUBIC YARDS PER HOUR; FITTED WITH IMPROVED RENEWABLE FACE-PLATES FOR
TUMBLERS AND DURABLE PINS AND BUSHINGS. RECORD—2½ YEARS' SERVICE
WITHOUT TAKING APART

A. W. ROBINSON, M, INST C E
MONTREAL CANADA

THIRTY-INCH HYDRAULIC DREDGE "SIMMONS"

A. W. ROBINSON, M. INST. C. E.
MONTREAL, CANADA

THE ROBINSON IMPROVED ROTARY CUTTER
FOR HEAVY CLAY SOILS.

A. W. ROBINSON, M. INST. C. E.
MONTREAL, CANADA.

MASSES OF STIFF CLAY DREDGED BY ROBINSON'S IMPROVED CUTTER AND
PUMPED THROUGH 2,000 FEET OF PIPE

A. W. ROBINSON M. INST C E
MONTREAL CANADA

THIRTY-SIX-INCH HYDRAULIC DREDGE "TARTE"
WORLD'S RECORD—750,000 CUBIC YARDS IN ONE MONTH
A. W. ROBINSON, M. INST. C.E.
MONTREAL, CANADA

FLOATING PIPE LINE FOR DREDGE "TARTE"
FITTED WITH ROBINSON'S PATENT BALL AND SOCKET SPRING JOINTS
FOR WITHSTANDING SEA WAVES

A. W. Robinson, M. Inst. C.E.
Montreal, Canada

3,500-HORSE POWER DREDGES "JINGA" AND "KALU"
FITTED WITH ROBINSON'S IMPROVED CUTTER AND SUCTION APPARATUS

A. W. ROBINSON, M. INST. C.E.
MONTREAL, CANADA

TWENTY-FOUR-INCH HYDRAULIC DREDGE "ALEXANDRA"
FITTED WITH ROBINSON'S IMPROVED CUTTER AND SUCTION APPARATUS

A. W. ROBINSON, M. INST. C.E.
MONTREAL, CANADA

HYDRAULIC DREDGE "PHARAON II"
FITTED WITH ROBINSON'S CUTTER
A. W. ROBINSON, M. INST. C.E.
MONTREAL, CANADA

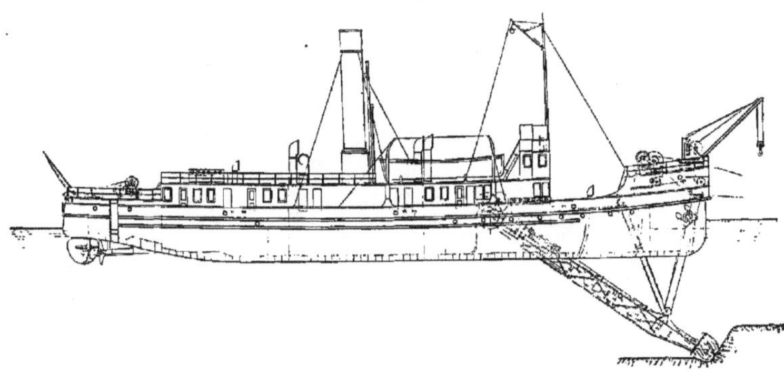

HYDRAULIC DREDGE "PHARAON II"
FITTED WITH ROBINSON'S CUTTER

A. W. ROBINSON, M. INST. C.E.
MONTREAL, CANADA

HYDRAULIC DREDGE "PHARAOH II"
FITTED WITH ROBINSON'S CUTTER

A. W. ROBINSON, M. Inst. C.E.
MONTREAL, CANADA

SELF-PROPELLING HYDRAULIC DREDGE "KING EDWARD"

A. W. Robinson, M. Inst. C.E.
Montreal, Canada

LIGHT-DRAFT SELF-PROPELLING FORWARD-FEED DREDGE "QUORRA"
CAPACITY: 1,000 CUBIC YARDS PER HOUR

A. W. Robinson, M. Inst C E
Montreal, Canada

TWENTY-INCH HYDRAULIC DREDGE
EXCAVATING ENTIRE PRISM OF CANAL AT ONE OPERATION. RECORD—229,00 CUBIC YARDS PER MONTH

A. W. ROBINSON, M. INST. C.E.
MONTREAL, CANADA

ONE OF FOUR LARGE LAND RECLAMATION DREDGES

A. W. ROBINSON, M. INST. C.E.
MONTREAL, CANADA

HYDRAULIC DREDGE ON UPPER WHITE NILE

A. W. ROBINSON M. INST C.E.
MONTREAL, CANADA

GRAB DREDGE, WORKING IN SUDD

A. W. ROBINSON, M. INST. C.E.
MONTREAL, CANADA.

SUSPENDED SHORE DISCHARGE OF HYDRAULIC DREDGE

A. W. ROBINSON, M. INST. C.E.
MONTREAL, CANADA

DIPPER DREDGE
TWELVE TONS EVERY FORTY SECONDS

A. W. Robinson, M. Inst. C.E.

FOUR-YARD DIPPER DREDGE
SHOWING ROBINSON'S PATENT BOOM AND DIRECT HOIST

FOUR-AND-A-HALF-YARD DIPPER DREDGE

FIVE-YARD DIPPER DREDGE

EIGHT-YARD DIPPER DREDGE "CAYO PIEDRA."

A. W. ROBINSON, M. INST. C.E.
MONTREAL, CANADA.

Mr. Robinson first began to develop the modern type of American shovel in 1886, and his designs are in use on all leading railroads and Public works, Panama Canal, etc. The above represents the latest type of shovel for railway use with direct wire rope hoist. Weight, 68 tons; lifting power, 23 tons; capacity of dipper, 2½ cubic yards; speed, 4 dippers per minute, or 20 cubic yards per minute.

A. W. ROBINSON, M. INST. C.E.
MONTREAL, CANADA

THREE-AND-A-HALF CUBIC FEET GOLD DREDGE

A. W. ROBINSON, M. INST. C.E.
MONTREAL, CANADA